Ready to Read
Rhyming Words

top

cat

mop

mat

How to Play

1. Press the Power button to turn the SD-X Reader on or off. The LED will light up when the SD-X Reader is on.

2. Touch the volume buttons found on this page to adjust the volume.

3. Touch words and pictures on the page to hear audio. The monkey gives instructions and starts activities.

4. After two minutes of inactivity, the SD-X Reader will beep and go to sleep.

5. If the batteries are low, the SD-X Reader will beep twice and the LED will start blinking. Replace the batteries by following the instructions on the next page. The SD-X Reader uses two AAA batteries.

6. To use headphones or earbuds, plug them into the headphone jack on the SD-X Reader.

Volume

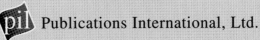

pil Publications International, Ltd.

Battery Information
Includes two replaceable AAA batteries (UM-4 or LR03).

Battery Installation
1. Open battery door with small flat-head or Phillips screwdriver.
2. Install new batteries according to +/- polarity. If batteries are not installed properly, the device will not function.
3. Replace battery door; secure with small screw.

Battery Safety
Batteries must be replaced by adults only. Properly dispose of used batteries. See battery manufacturer for disposal recommendations. Do not mix alkaline, standard (carbon-zinc), or rechargeable (nickel-cadmium) batteries. Do not mix old and new batteries. Only recommended batteries of the same or equivalent type should be used. Remove weakened or dead batteries. Never short-circuit the supply terminals. Non-rechargeable batteries are not to be recharged. Do not use rechargeable batteries. If batteries are swallowed, in the USA, promptly see a doctor and have the doctor phone 1-202-625-3333 collect. In other countries, have the doctor call your local poison control center. This product uses 2 AAA batteries (2 X 1.5V = 3.0 V). Use batteries of the same or equivalent type as recommended. The supply terminals are not to be short-circuited. Batteries should be changed when sounds mix, distort, or become otherwise unintelligible as batteries weaken. The electrostatic discharge may interfere with the sound module. If this occurs, please simply restart the sound module by pressing any key.

In Europe, the dustbin symbol indicates that batteries, rechargeable batteries, button cells, battery packs, and similar materials must not be discarded in household waste. Batteries containing hazardous substances are harmful to the environment and to health. Please help to protect the environment from health risks by telling your children to dispose of batteries properly and by taking batteries to local collection points. Batteries handled in this manner are safely recycled.

Warning: Changes or modifications to this unit not expressly approved by the party responsible for compliance could void the user's authority to operate the equipment.

NOTE: This equipment has been tested and found to comply with the limits for a Class B digital device, pursuant to Part 15 of the FCC Rules. These limits are designed to provide reasonable protection against harmful interference in a residential installation. This equipment generates, uses, and can radiate radio frequency energy and, if not installed and used in accordance with the instructions, may cause harmful interference to radio communications. However, there is no guarantee that interference will not occur in a particular installation. If this equipment does cause harmful interference to radio or television reception, which can be determined by turning the equipment off and on, the user is encouraged to try to correct the interference by one or more of the following measures: Reorient or relocate the receiving antenna. Increase the separation between the equipment and receiver. Connect the equipment into an outlet on a circuit different from that to which the receiver is connected. Consult the dealer or an experienced radio TV technician for help.

Contributing Writers: Natalie Goldstein, Anne Schreiber, Kristen Walsky, Michele Warrence-Schreiber

Consultants: Susan A. Miller, Ed.D., Dr. Leslie Ann Perry, Dr. Elizabeth C. Stull

Illustrators: Nicholas Myers, James Schlottman, George Ulrich

Picture Credits: Art Explosion; Comstock RF; Corbis RF; Image Club Graphics; PhotoDisc; PIL Collection; Shutterstock; StockByte

Louis Weber, C.E.O., Publications International, Ltd.
7373 North Cicero Avenue
Lincolnwood, Illinois 60712

Ground Floor, 59 Gloucester Place
London W1U 8JJ

Customer Service:
1-888-724-0144 or customer_service@pilbooks.com
www.pilbooks.com

SD-X Interactive is a registered trademark in the United States and Canada.

Manufactured in China.

8 7 6 5 4 3 2 1
ISBN-10: 1-4508-2063-8
ISBN-13: 978-1-4508-2063-9

Rhyming Pictures

A **rhyme** is when two words have the same sound at the end.

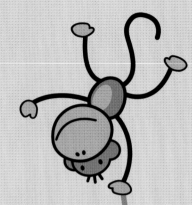

Rhyming
Pictures

Identify rhyming sounds.

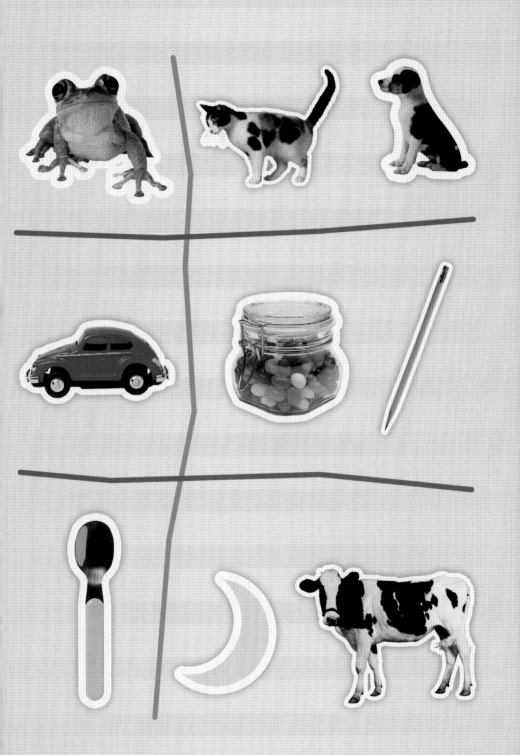

Rhyme Time

Identify rhyming words in print.

bag

flag

Do
They
Rhyme?

mop

box

sled

bug

hug **fun**

bed **food**

mouse

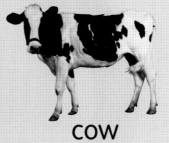

cow

now **not**

nose **house**

ball

sink

tall **bag**

wink **sing**

Rhyme Time

Identify rhyming sounds.

Rhyme or Not?

Identify rhyming words in print.

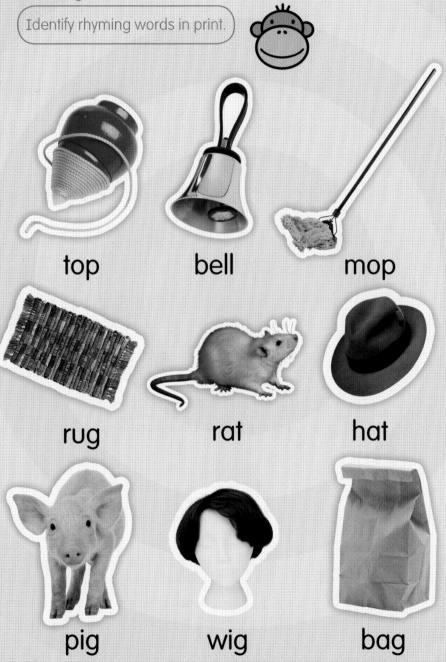

top

bell

mop

rug

rat

hat

pig

wig

bag

Rhyme Me a Poem

Identify rhyming words in poems.

I have a cat,
who sits on a mat.
He ate cookies and cake,
in the sand by the lake.
He liked to lie in the sun,
Now he's so big, he can't even run.

A Fat Cat

Identify the **at** word family.

Adding different letters in front of the word ending **at** makes different words.

The Man Ran

Identify the **an** word family.

You can put different letters in front of the word ending **an**.

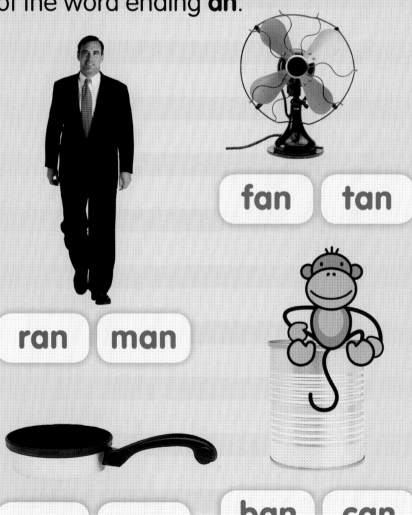

fan tan

ran man

pan van

ban can

Ten Men and a Hen

I am a chicken.
I lay eggs.
I am a

pen | **hen**

I am a number.
I come after the
number nine.
I am a

ten | **when**

I am more than
one man.
I am a group of

then | **men**

The Pet Is Wet

I take my **pet** to visit the

I have not **yet** flown in a

I always get **wet** when I fish with a

The Pin Is Thin

Identify the **in** word family.

The man has freckles on his skin. He has a thin chin. He has a great big grin.

The Ring Is the Thing

Identify the **ing** word family.

I am pretty.
You wear me on your finger.
I am a

ring **wing**

You sit on me.
You move me
back and forth.
I am a

swing **ding**

A Cub in a Tub

Identify the **ub** and **ug** word families.

Don't Block the Clock

Identify the **ock** word family.

block

rock

clock

lock

sock

A Sad Fad

Stay and Play

Identify the **ay** word family.

hay

baby

jay

day

play

clay

may

fly

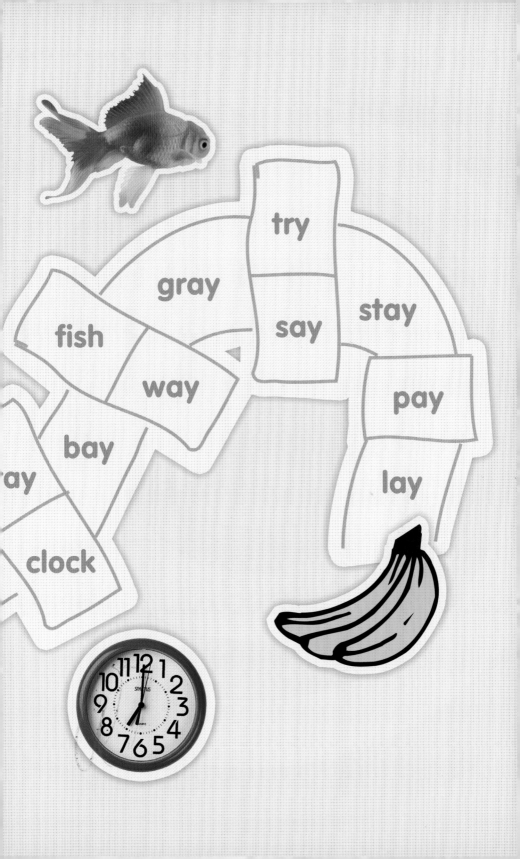

Oh Well

The shell they were trying
to sell fell into the well!
Ring the bell! Who can we tell?

Word Switch

Identify the **ill** word family.

 _ill

 _ill

 _ill

p **b** **h**

Family Friends

Hickory dickory dock.
The mouse ran up the clock.

The sled is red.

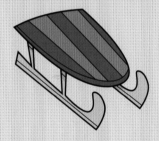

The cop said stop.

There's a fat rat on the mat.